Praise for *The House That Fire Built*

Glaser's writing beautifully balances the uncanny atmosphere of the house's haunted memories and the devastating aftermath of the fire with moments of radical vulnerability, making the emotional stakes of the story deeply personal as this family turns devastating loss into a bridge for healing and insight. *The House That Fire Built* invites readers to walk through the fire of life with a wise, courageous practice in mind—to be a witness to our lives moment by moment and cross the threshold of suffering, no matter how painful that might be. This skillfully crafted collection of poems weaves a tale of resilience, redemption, and forgiveness that deepens our sense of humanity.

—Juan Velasco-Moreno, author of *Massacre of the Dreamers*

In an era when giant California wildfires often dominate the news, Glaser's shocking fire—and ghost—story is uniquely personal, so eerie that its haunting imagery and fearsome narrative are seared into my memory like a horror movie. Read it if you enjoy good poetry, and a good scare, knowing the hero survives: "Let be demon fire that saved us from a future / shadowed in nightmare." I feel certain that Edgar Allen Poe would have appreciated *The House That Fire Built*.

—April Ossmann, author of *We*

Compelling, accessible, and remarkably honest, *The House That Fire Built* is filled with stark, realistic poems that paint an intimate portrait of loss, family, and the ever-present need for empathy. Each poem maps out the human heart in relation to that larger earth heart, in all their internal conflicts, with precision and grace, imbuing the smallest human details with authenticity and layered meanings. Overflowing with vivid and accessible language, *The House That Fire Built* is both intellectually stimulating and emotionally engaging, reminding us of the beautiful complexities of being human.

—John Sibley Williams, author of *Scale Model of a Country at Dawn*

Part narrative mystery, part meditation on loss, trust and acceptance, *The House That Fire Built* toggles between literal and figurative fire with dextrous verse and vivid storytelling. As I read, I kept recalling the relayed dialectic early in the book—"Abundance. Futility. / What is wished for. / What is."—and how it informs so much of our experience. Glaser proposes, "After fire and dust/what is a life?" As I came to the end, I had my own questions: Can grief at once be caused by fire and be the fire itself? What are the true sources that ignite the fires in our lives? And where will asking such questions even lead? The beauty of this book lies in its awareness that wisdom is ultimately evidenced in our queries, not our decrees.

—MIAH JEFFRA, author of *American Gospel*

The House That Fire Built

Poems

THE HOUSE THAT FIRE BUILT

Poems

Kirk Glaser

MadHat Press
Cheshire, Massachusetts

MadHat Press
MadHat Incorporated
PO Box 422, Cheshire, MA 01225

Copyright © 2025 Kirk Glaser
All rights reserved.

The Library of Congress has assigned
this edition a Control Number of
2025942020

ISBN 978-1-952335-99-0 (paperback)

Words by Kirk Glaser
Cover image by Rhiannon Janeschild
Cover design by Marc Vincenz

www.MadHat-Press.com

First Printing
Printed in the United States of America

for Miranda

to walk through the fire
to shed leaves of ash
to plant seeds from flame
to stay the path
together

Table of Contents

i The House Dreams

I Breathe	3
The House of Inheritance	5
Clearing the Field	7
The House Dreams	10
Under Currents	14
Storm Forecast	15
Tapping	17

ii What's Left on the Tongue

The House Cards	21
Freeway Con	24
The Mask	27
The Dying Man	29
Too Late	33
What's Left on the Tongue	36
Indian Cove	38
The Crossing, I	39
The Crossing, II	41
The Crossing, III	48
Cremation	50

iii Fingers of Flame

White Courtesy Telephone	55
First Loss	58
Fire and Wine	60
The Stranger	62
Ground Vision	65
Wires Like Snakes	67
Found	71
A Mother's Craft	73

The Altar Stones	75
Fire Inspector	77
1. Incident Report	
2. Interrogation	
3. Illumination	
Timepiece	84
Fingers of Flame	85
Night Ploy	88

iv Leave It Alone

One of Everything	93
The Crone	95
Leave It Alone	98
Fire Insurance	101
Telephone Call	103
A Reckoning	106
The Café of Lost Confessions	111
The Angels and Devas Debate Karmic Parameters in the Cloudy World of Mortals	117

v Inheritance of Fire

Song in Cinders	123
Swailing Field	124
The Live Oaks' Fire Song	126
Inheritance of Fire	128
Irritant in the Solution	130
A Leaf of Ash	132
Fire's Way	134
The House That Fire Built	136

Notes	139
Acknowledgments	141
About the Author	143

*Sometimes the Angel of God
saves us from the fire
sometimes through the fire
and sometimes not at all.*

THE HOUSE DREAMS

I Breathe

Reek in the doorway
when we enter the house
a waft from rotten
teeth in the mouth
                I swell
We scrub log walls
seal cracks in floors
open windows wide
still flinch at threshold
stench clinging
like oil to skin
forgotten pound of meat
behind cellar door
                I seep
Each unknown to
each we dream a woman
in the kitchen 3AM
who hums who leans
speared on a rod womb
blood swirling into batter
she folds with a spoon
baking cookies for no one
                I cling
A man at the table
who stitches mouths shut
wife and sons
slumped in chairs
                Pass through me
We burn sage
smudge each room

offer prayers for the dead
as if pungent smoke
will close what seethes
what hoards hurt creased
in forgotten skin
                If you dare

In the house of dream
desire cracks walls
sets hooks under skin
and pulls us in
                To enter my breath

The House of Inheritance

"Why are you stopping, Daddy?"
our daughter asks from the back.
"Look, a deer and her fawn."

Last month three followed, barely able to step.
Did the doe love them distantly, knowing
one would feed the cougar, another shatter

across blind steel on the human road?
This third, spotless now, tracking her steps
may outlive its first year. Does the doe's heart

open? Or did it break and break, free
of illusion that a world assembled by choice
and plan creates order safe from chance.

*

What have we been given
in your father's death?
At a party, the tarot's tease:

Abundance. Futility.
What is wished for.
What is.

*

Alone I drive the mountain to the house
above the bay, your father's before trumped
by cancer. Winding down the driveway,

Kirk Glaser

ruminating on boxes to unpack,
a cold poison spills behind my eyes—
wife and daughter hang from meat hooks,

blood spattered on walls, dripping to oak floors.
Breathe, shake my head, run hands over the wheel,
make it pass before terror clots the mind.

Why each time I turn down the drive,
this vision, forgotten, thrusts me into
a house of devastation? The chill of being

plucked like a string, a charred hand hovering
to play its single chord, a diminished key.
Futility, Abundance: luck is a neutral country

where we inherit what we fail to perceive.
I kill the engine, climb from the car.
Our daughter jumps from her trike

and runs to me under great live oaks,
the home we make where garden touches forest
cascading to the sea, her joy splintering

my mind's perversities, and again
I forget to tell you,
until fire takes the home.

Clearing the Field

Gabe, the hired hand, hops on the mower's tail
and grabs my shoulders to weigh down wheels
spinning dust high on the dry weed slope.

Sheer morning gladness at the brim, no reason
to feel hands slide round my neck, fingers
dig in. I shake it off, slip the throttle to full,

drop the blade to clear the field.
Spirit fire far from home and be done
with him leaning on my back.

Later, on the slope under the big oak's shade
eating lunch, dust-coated, shirts sweat soaked,
Gabe nods at the red mower in the truck's bed:

"You could start a business with those." What is it
in his voice tingeing the fact? How need shapes thought,
how possession thrusts itself between two men

who work together, whether they work together or apart.
"You work pretty hard, for a guy like you."
He leans against the trunk, chewing open-mouthed.

A dust devil stirs out of the field and blows
through us. Sting of metal in the nose,
of blood in the mouth. A burnt hand reaching ...

I walk to the tailgate, slam it shut.
"Wind's kicking up, too hot to work anymore."
"Sorry, just meant, you don't need to, right?

Your some kind of writer, teacher? Must be
a good life." I pull at the tie-downs on the mower.
"I need to pick up my daughter at school."

Gabe rises, lights a cigarette, the flame a ghost
flaring under the sun as he draws it in.
He holds the pack out, I shake my head, he smiles,

"Yeah, figured. Listen, I've got this screenplay
all worked out. What do you think? Two guys,
a girl, no money, sick of their jobs. They rip off

a resort and go on the run, but she falls for one.
They double-cross the other guy and split.
Police chopper chases them off a cliff, the car

a big ball of flame. Great movie, huh? Just need
to bang it out. All it takes is money and the balls
to make people do what you want." Gabe stretches,

faces the house. "We could use this place for the party scene,
booze and drugs and people all night. The jealous guy
finds the couple in bed, dumps his bottle on the sheets

and throws a match. They escape and he's left there
with nothing, the fire raging." I open the door.
"Action, love story, betrayal, it's all there,"

and slip into the seat. Just the words
on the page that will never get written.
"See you tomorrow, I'll pay you then."

And be done with you. The engine roars,
the AC blows its sober cold.
He grows small in the mirror as I wind up

the road, still standing by the house,
taking in the view. Maybe he's harmless,
just gassing, maybe it's all in my head.

Kirk Glaser

The House Dreams

You push at the swollen door
to reach a dying father.

Light spits through jambs,
the knob turns. "Who's there?"

you call, seizing it, your hand
seared by a rod of flame.

The door bulges to swallow you,
laughter scorching the frame,

a voice from within

              I control what happens here

*

My hand an iron pipe,
I strike the creature, thud upon

thud, drumbeat of charred leather
skin traveling up my arm

to clot my throat with iron and salt
and still I pound

back and skull,
legs and arms

The House That Fire Built

stop it
stop it   crawling

across the scorched field,
dirt blind eyes, clotted mouth,

silt oozing from its ears.
I pound until it crackles upright,

staggers toward me
dirt spilling from its mouth

as I reach for the door

                I am   what rises here

*

A metal rod spears a woman's belly,
out her back, pinning her slumped

over the kitchen sink, apron oozing
red. Once owned by the house,

she washes metal pans, meticulous
in her pain to lift and wipe each clean.

Water swells the sink, spills over her torso
pink across the floor, flooding the house

as cookies bake for no child in the home

        I am what happened here

*

A rod glistens on the kitchen counter
the night your father swallows pills

and fails to die. You lift it, a ragged
hand grips the other end,

fingers welded, you can't let go,
thrown to the wall, heaved

to the high ceiling and dropped,
the creature sliding you

into the hole at the core of its being

        I am what pierces here

*

The door holds fast to a room of toys
and books and little girl's dresses,

a grandmother's childhood bed,
where a daughter sleeps

through her parents' dreams,
light licking under the door

The House That Fire Built

to the music of breaking glass

I am   what follows here

Kirk Glaser

Under Currents

When the body dies
does memory flicker out
like light   when the filament
breaks in a worn bulb

And suffering   does it cease
at life's close   or surge
like a current snapping
frayed strands   those who remain
holding the ends

What is suffering   but memory
caught in the spinning blades
a life that flickers
through hallways   rooms
                Or is seized by what inhabits
to the last breath
                the house   darkness that eats light
when it sputters out
                to feed a desperate flame

Storm Forecast

Hawk-beaked, fierce-eyed,
we circle the house, hail
from our wings battering
the windows in warning
as the last threads
unravel and lay bare
the father's bitten soul.

> *this house   mine*
> *I scratch at doors*
> *oil-soaked fingers*
> *kindle cracks in walls*
> *I see you gyre   waiting*
> *as I scrabble below floors*
> *on cold limbs forged*
> *of matter's absence*
> *you can do nothing*
> *to nothing*

True, we can only take
in our beak a thread offered
by the dying's hand,
cannot sway the force
that sucks light from the atom.
You, creature, hunt
whoever steps into the nothing
storm whose course is set
by father death.

Kirk Glaser

                    eater of light   I am
                    I finger into my maw
                    knotted cords   pain   lies
                    twists of bitter pleasure
                    that drop from dying flesh
                    I devour   I thicken
                    with suffering

So we must let
the house be seized,
cold hands gather
the dying man.
We hover to draw horror,
if we can, away from those
caught in the wake.

Tapping

Mother and daughter dancing   Behind them crack
before corner mirrors   the basement
     room to ease   the cellar door
dying   hours away
                                        swing it wide
silky wig   on daughter's head
shirt glistens   sequins   roll stale breeze across the floor
       hanging to ankles
size four taps   on tiny feet   tongue of air   flicking embers

Together you dance   toward the dancers   who dance
to Madonna   laughing
toes and heels   clatter   not watching
      on cold concrete
                                  door open on door
You watch   your daughter
      watch herself   the flat vacuum of mirror
mirror inside   mirror
              girl   after girl   sealed around them
growing smaller
                      into nothing

What's Left on the Tongue

The House Cards

A party to celebrate the new neighbor,
your father, house perched on the summit
facing the bay, a million-dollar view away
from ours nestled one ridge west.
Redwoods and firs drop down canyon walls,
dark spires netting stars in branches
over the lights of Santa Cruz.

A magician by the window pulls coins
from air, guesses cards to light applause.
"Who brought him?" I ask. You nod at Don's
latest lover. "Bea did, the fortune teller, too."
A woman sits at a table, guest's hand in hers
palm up over a dark velvet spread.
The magician's smile drops, he stiffens, intoning
a hunger smothers the house, stifles his magic.
A hand flips open a fan to sweep evil spirits
away, fueling laughter. He takes a bow.

The woman calls your name, come, sit,
shuffles the tarot, Crowley's dark deck.
I pull up a chair as you touch three cards
from the spread in her hand: Sorrow she lays
center, bound by the Tower and Death.
Her fingers hover over them like moth wings
close to a flame. She touches Sorrow's
three swords stabbing the rose,
petals falling through steel-black folds
into darkness: "The swords piercing the heart:

confusion of intellect, freedom lacking
guidance, sowing discord, deceit."

You glance at Don sunk in an armchair,
wine glass in hand. His face pale, eyes dull,
impresario lost in a stupor, not feeding
on the crowd spinning his tales
of fallen stars snared to perform for him
pennies on the days when gilded
by Hollywood, Broadway, Vegas.

"Here, center, to be tempered
by the cards that flank it." The tarot reader
taps her finger on charcoal-boned Death,
steel cords strung to femur, scythe a shuttle
weaving through a helix loom
suspending the womb-curled dead.
"Death is change, to end, to begin, only
by letting go what is worn out.
Here, by Sorrow, the rose reborn,
abundance: coming into wealth, your father
moving here to be near you, your family."

"And here," the woman hurries on, "purification
through fire," pointing to the Tower.
Carbon-facet bodies leap from walls
crumbling toward a maw belching sword-flames
that slice the entry door. "What is rigid collapses
into new beginnings. Sorrow transformed
by this home on the mountain."

The House That Fire Built

Laughter and clapping behind her,
another successful trick. Glasses clink.
You glance my way, back down at the cards.
I stare, too: the mouth of flame, the bloody rose,
the scythe a hook to a dream flickering
in the back of my skull, scattered as fingers
slip the three cards back into the deck,
quick as a spider snipping a bundle
from its web. "Let's go have a glass of wine.
Don, your father, he's a lucky man."

I feel you feel the gulf of what is left   *To grasp*
unsaid, the ocean's dark mass below the windows   *what you seek*
spread across the bay as if to swallow   *the cards*
the far lights dotting the base of the Santa Lucias *betray nothing*
a faint glow of fog-snuffed Monterey   *that is not there*
                              and the nothing that abides.

Freeway Con

Winding down the steep grade
to the hospital for tests.
Don buckled in back
calls from the silence,
*Watch for the straightaway
ahead. CHP sets traps
where it's easy to open up.*
Your lips tighten,
knuckles white on the wheel.

His cancer-tamped murmur
floats against engine and wind:
*Last year sailing down here
a cop pulled me over,
stuck his face in my window,
found me sobbing. I told him,
My wife, she's dying of cancer,
I have to get to the hospital.
Pull it together, he said,
drive slower. I sat there
ten minutes before the shaking
stopped enough to drive.*

You stare through the mirror
at your father slumped against the door,
eyes closed, a shadow smile,
bloated belly strapped to the seat,
glance at me as if asking:
Did I hear right? Did he hear
himself? Or obscure to him

The House That Fire Built

as a dream told fresh from the sheets,
its meaning a fish that shimmers
before it darts into depths.

We snake down the road
where in a flash of red and blue
he devised a tale to use your mother
—the woman cheated on,
committed for depression, buried
after swallowing a bottle of pills—
to dodge a ticket.

This con man, what made him
take pleasure in crafting poses
to flummox agents, sway performers,
always gain the upper hand? Or deceive
a wife, cajole your brothers, you
to command the family show.

Was it being lone kid on the road
with his mother singing clubs
through Depression and war,
pulled from schools, dumped
backstage or in bars with strangers,
forced to keep his guard,
play his smarts, run a scam
that bent him to mimic and trick?

Drifting asleep that night,
you turn to me, his story

Kirk Glaser

    rendered clear after a day
    of freeway noise: how his body
    chewed on lies, shook him
    to his core— conned by his cancer
    already feeding on his liver
    a year ago, the Thanksgiving
    meal, the habitual bottle of Bordeaux,
    when he collapsed, confessing to all,
    I'm not well.

The Mask

"Wait here a minute,"
Don tells his granddaughter,

waddles into the closet,
jumps out wearing an orange wig,

rubber elephant trunk
over nose, a fluorescent Ganesh

prancing the bedroom,
fingers curled like tusks

at the corners of his mouth.
Grunting more like a pig,

you think as Rhiannon steps
back, grabs your leg.

"Stop, you're scaring her!"
Arm across your daughter's

chest, his antics miscued.
"It's just Grandfather, sweetie."

But the urge to know what is
real, what illusion, to laugh

or cry, whatever this beast
proves to be, pulls her

to snatch the snout, let go.
It snaps back. Don snorts

and Rhiannon giggles. You sigh
as he dances some more

before hands grab swollen
belly, the jostled liver.

The mask falls and he
drops to the bed.

The Dying Man

puts his house in order
    from a living
  room chair   deals out
properties   cars   furniture
    down to photos   old LPs

His mind struggles
      acid blood   failing liver
to dictate lists   between spells
  you unsure
whether sleep   or quiet
    rumination
a man diving
        past pain
    the turgid flow
  in veins   grabbing at strands
    of fraying self
impresario   father
  businessman   lover

Eyes flicker   head lifts
  did I tell you
    I had Chris declared dead

Yes   you did   you don't say
  when driving him up the coast
past Devil's Slide   boulders
  overhead
      ocean below
a tear on his cheek

        you crested the ridge
   and he slid the moment
behind the rock of a joke

As now   a hand lifted
   in mock benediction
I want you to celebrate
   a wake   a month after I die
      the best wine   a good caterer
we Indians want a party
   when we go

You pull your grimace into a smile
   a quarter Oneida   his mother's side
      fractioned   bloodline played
to cow a roomful of white men
   cutting deals   even try to outwit
      Death   pinning
Chronicle headline on his office wall
   "Indian Roars Back to Life"
      photo of the resurrected bike
         cutout of Don
         taped to its seat

*

Winter light   late afternoon   stories come
   Indian grandfather
     the guy could lift a piano
   orphan boy   wandering as winter set in
   with children and women

THE HOUSE THAT FIRE BUILT

barefoot   ragged clothes
   survived the massacres
taken to a reservation
   with Iroquois and Ojibwa
escaped to Toronto
   met a Scottish girl

She arrived in New York
   a change of clothes   an iron kettle
   all she had   once her husband
   walked from the boat
   and into the crowd
indentured herself   fled beatings
   found her life with an Oneida man

Don waves at a shelf of photos
   that one   the two of them   see?
old wire frame   a wedding pair
   faded albumen print
     heavy frock   stiff laced dress
    man tall   broad   dark-skinned
woman fair and narrow   a bony strength
   they never married   he smiles
took it to stop questions   hung it on their wall
   screw the white man's law

*

On Christmas Eve   he forces a hand
to open a bottle of Margaux
twenty-five years old

Kirk Glaser

a great year   been saving it
    let's see if it passes the test
he drops the cork
    it stands on end
    he chuckles and pours
for daughter   son-in-law   girlfriend
    nothing   for himself
   nothing   but he fills
with light as he watches us lift
    deep red globes   the ripe old wine
      to salute him
              in his closing circle

Too Late

*Miranda, is there anything
you'd like to know
about your mother?*
A father's voice floating through rooms
as you prepare dinner
and windows rattle,
a squall blowing over the ridge.

Anything you would like
to know unraveling
the final thread of him
back to that house
of lies and broken tables,
the women who came and went
through doors closed to you.

You cut carrots and kale,
thigh and leg for his soup,
don't ask: What about
the night Mom came naked
to my bed? When she pulled
me to the floor, hugging me
and crying, "I hate men,
I hate them all." Her breath
a box of alcohol and pills
closing in on her.
"Only you only you I love."

What happened when you
dragged her away?

Kirk Glaser

The next morning
blinds drawn in her room,
door light slanting
across her face when I peeked in,
a black eye swollen shut.
While downstairs you played
show tunes, flipped pancakes,
squeezed oranges into bright cut glass.

Did you think twice
about commititng her
to an asylum? About dragging
me and Ben and Chris
past women talking to walls,
slamming heads into palms,
to stand by her bedridden,
branded with straps?
Your smiles and pleasantries,
her swollen face, chapped lips
struggling to form *Miranda*.

Why did you never utter a word
to explain what I saw?

A dish from the oven
cracks in your hand,
a door slams shut
from a draft. Your father silent
in the next room.

The House That Fire Built

The house swells, breathing
in gusts of storm,
swallowing questions.
Where to begin,
how to grasp this cruel offering
too belated to be a gift?

What's Left on the Tongue

You stir the broth to feed him,
salt and season a wariness to
how the heart can open

as his body fails,
a desert flower fed by storms
before washed away.

You who rose a wilderness
around yourself far from his words
that ground two sons to madness,

carved a maze around his wife
who found her way out
through an amber bottle of pills.

All this the house sucks in,
exhales a rot through walls,
while you dare dream

one last chance to learn
what *father* means. You step
to the clearing's edge, the slash

and burn, feet testing for snares,
surprised to find compassion,
a dry root fed by blood

THE HOUSE THAT FIRE BUILT

flowing through you both,
what you offer spoonful by
spoonful into his mouth.

For years you walked fields of anger,
of fire and blackened earth.
You will walk them again.

Indian Cove

Final night of consciousness,
one last story: rowing a boat
with his mother an afternoon
between shows at a dance club
where she sang all summer
for a big band.

They were everywhere then,
lots of gigs for musicians.
Nineteen thirty-nine, maybe forty,
this posh Connecticut town.
No war yet, but you could hear it
behind everything adults said.
His father conductor gone,
too drunk to lead a band.

The two of them rowing away
an afternoon in the Sound,
a perfect boy's day, green light
shining through leaves,
sun suspended in humid air,
salt and mud and pitch
stinging the nose.
One hand in cool water,
the other conducting
the song she sang, her voice
just for him.

The Crossing, I

His final bid to skirt the passage,
a bottle of pills rattling in hand.

Beyond words, he motions you
to place them in his mouth. By the bed

you stand, a wave-battered rock,
only your head turning side to side.

All his will to spill them in his palm,
cup the vessels as they are tossed

by the trembling surge of fingers.
He raises them to mouth, hand drops,

a dead wife grips his wrist
holding him to the torpor of his pain.

A modern, no dread of the nothing
he presumes on the other side,

no fantasy of ancestors or angels,
only indignity he fears:

*Not the way my mother suffered, months
in that hospital hooked to machines.*

Home, lots of morphine, his last demand,
the powder coin to speed the crossing.

He tries to lift pills to his mouth again,
calculating numbers in nonsense sums:

How many do I need to fill the sail?
How many to scuttle the ship?

They spill across the sheets,
minnows darting from his reach.

Fingers flounder blindly for white
on white, until the hand falls still.

The Crossing, II

Over dark waters
      my body floats   a ship of pain
      constrained
            by morphine holds

seized
      by moss-bone fingers   steering where
      I fear
all that I wrestle   all I have wrought will

            Jane
reach out your hand
      take mine
            are you by my bed
with Miranda
    or here
      floating in this bloodpulse sea

        No
hand me that bottle of pills
        come out of the weeping courtroom
    cut the words I coiled
      around you
  unsound in mind   *incompetent*
            until they snaked
down your throat
    all just a ploy   don't you see   just a game
like the promises   the pianos and horses

Kirk Glaser

     never kept
to win the children from you

Please peel off that swollen face
eyes flattened like foil
   no don't turn from me don't sink
     back into the waters take me with you
                Jane

*

Christopher my first born
         son
  standing on the mud bank.

Read me a poem play your guitar for your old man dying
             my hope of hope

    No not the words that split your tongue
    on their broken glass the ones
      I kicked aside
      called teen-age bluster

I hear demons
  in my head
    I want a priest
  I want an exorcist
      I want to get them out

Schizophrenic a diagnosis a word
  to clasp

        too late
                your hands fists
my face a wall
    prescriptions
    restrictions
    threats
    police

You disappeared   wandered
        preaching the Word
until a call
    a prison cell in Spain
    I brought you home
              hope
upon hope
    more doctors   treatments

Their pills the Devil's
            instrument
conspiring against the Messiah
    they numb
    my Vision

This final decade   silence
             never
    to behold my son again

Yes   I see the paper
    you chew   Declaration of Death
        my signature   ink bleeding

Kirk Glaser

                down your chin
                      only to protect
        all I made   of this world
for your sister   don't you see
                      the only one to survive

      Survive you, you mouth
No
      Christopher   please don't turn away
      stay by my side
            read me one of your poems
or *The Four Quartets*
      you used to recite from memory

No   not now
The Wasteland
                  spilling
      from your lips   an unreal city

*

Miranda   is it you
                your warm hand
    holding me   as phantoms weave through mists
      wife and son
                dissolving

The dark sea churns
      a creature roils   beneath my bloated mass
          slippery hands seize
    a face   a body   mine

THE HOUSE THAT FIRE BUILT

                a ship of entrails   sinking into the
                      nothing that waits
Is this morphine's trick
               or the final crossing

                      Miranda
                      help me
        my last
joy
     you stayed by my side   bathed this body
prepared my way
        come closer   let me tell you
                    are my lips moving
I couldn't hear
          when you were young
how Chris locked you in closets
      pressed a knife to your throat
                       as he preached
     fire and salvation
                  I couldn't fathom the letters
you wrote
     to lead me back
          to your mother's funeral
  the obituary you showed Chris
    clipped from the local paper
          never meant   to be seen
Mother
     dead from pills
                not a failed heart
the story I fed you

Kirk Glaser

      the first thread cut in Chris' mind
          adults are liars   never to be trusted

What did I know
    of his anger
      how you who suffered
scarcely home   or upstairs   closed doors
      women's laughter and moans

while you   a girl   below
made meals   no one
    came to eat
set plates for Sunday brunch
  a table   I threw over
to show my son   who controlled
      the house of rage

*

Could it have been   not just
    a mother's broken gene
              that tore my son
tore us all   apart
        Could it have been
a current I created
      a swell   this creature rides
    clutching   to drown my heart
      devour memories

the happy ones   minnows too slippery to catch
    in my swollen hands

The House That Fire Built

              unable to lash them to my chest
for the final crossing
                    a daughter swinging in my arms
on the beach   young son on my shoulders
     the eldest leading the way
             down a path of oaks and bays
                    on a fall day with nothing to do

     the smell of the lakeside
           Jane's skin   when we first kissed

     sparks of light   pinched and snuffed

a wife's eyes stare   cold embers
            above a mouth stitched shut
a son's body rises
       from a heap in a ditch   where the unreal city
            eats at the water's edge

           and I sink
                  into oil-soaked mud

What do I leave in my wake

The Crossing, III

We circle the bed with a few close friends,
strands of kelp entangled in the rising sea.
Rhiannon darts between us, minnow flash

too young to understand end, yet she slows
by the bed, takes our hands to hold against
the strange current pulling her grandfather

down. Days past awareness, or so we believe.
Lungs rattle with black sputum, the liver failed,
toxins filling vessels. The body swells

as if to trap the sea that made a life,
resist the crossing. But water pushes against
cell walls, ceaseless, seeking way to stasis.

Hour after hour we float, exhausted,
you whisper in your father's ear a sea air,
"Let go, find the current, leave."

Watery lungs rasp, chest lifts the sheet,
a stillness distending until lungs collapse.
Then a gentle rise and fall.

Was it the murmur of your voice,
words like buoys clanging in a dark cove
that set his body rocking on steady seas?

*

The House That Fire Built

Outside, the scent of trees lashed by rain,
cold earth, I gulp air as if breaking surface.
A hawk circles the winter house, pivoting

tail in a vortex of mist to vanish in cloud.
The mind, the soul, a feathered hope,
what rides the currents of watery tissues,

what in him resists? Does the dying mind
hoard its ruins, prop a stone threshold up
with the final staves of desire?

A dream returns, or is it a wish,
a hawk-winged angel, fierce eye hovering
over your father, claws piercing the muscle

of his heart between its final thump and
the forever after, carries him off
on the breath that relinquishes the thread.

Until then, he must suffer the body.

Kirk Glaser

Cremation

After fire and dust
   what is a life?
Memory and nothing,
   the past an urn on a shelf—
all compelled to walk the path
   through the cold ash forest,
sloughing the triumphs
   and ruins of a few years.

Against what you inherit
   is it enough to hold
our child, touch lips,
   dig hands into earth,
set them to work
   for pure sake of serving
moment upon moment?

Is it enough to sow
   into the slagheap
of the past and smother
   what reaches for us—
a seed, pyriscent,
   waiting in dry bone powder
for fire to crack the urn-shell,
   twist roots into the house
foundation, sprout fingers
   of a seared hand.

Enough to sate
 what eats at this world
flowering rust and ash?

Fingers of Flame

White Courtesy Telephone, Detroit Metropolitan Airport

On the ground for a layover,
    summoned by terminal speakers,
        cold hand holding my daughter's,
           a voice in my ear.
Who?   Gabe?   Who?
        Oh. How did you find me?
        Why are you calling?

I was heading up early
to check on things,
    knew you were flying home.
I saw a firetruck
        coming down the road
and got this awful feeling.

When I saw the place,
    firetrucks and people and smoke
all this smoke, the house
    black and burnt

all your dreams,
    I couldn't believe it,
        all your things.
        That beautiful home.

What?   The house?   What happened?

Gone.

A fire.
        It's all gone.

The shaking begins, bones leaching time
    crumbling into what
        will be, what will not be.
I squeeze my daughter's hand,
    look down, smile,
    the blood drains
from the mask of my face.

All night long I couldn't sleep,
        kept feeling something wrong.

What do you mean   all gone?
        What did you do Gabe?

Nothing's left   a few charred logs
    spiked together
        leaning over the foundation.
The fire marshall kept staring at them.
    Alligatoring, he called it,
        the way the fire crawled up the corners
    like they'd just been oiled.
No, I told him, just the decks,
I'd been there yesterday
    staining the decks.

You were there? What? We told you
    not while we were away. What did you do?

The House That Fire Built

I asked could it be the rags
    I stuffed in a can, the oily tarps
        I left in the garage.
Maybe, he said, maybe
    spontaneous combustion.
        Oh god, I'm so sorry,
what's happened to you,   what's happening.
I hope it wasn't my fault
        I had to let you know
before you saw.
    Miranda, is she there with you?

What? She's on the plane.
Why does he ask? Disembodied voice
    of a stranger who kept showing up,
asking for work,
sat down for dinner
    one night his truck wouldn't start,
played hide and seek with our daughter.

Oh I'm so sorry
    it's the worst thing
in the world   what's happened.
    I'm so glad I caught you.

First Loss

Strapped in   the fuselage
    after Gabe's call
the first loss   to bite the mind

the journal   written
    to our daughter
the cover   black and white

photo   one day old
    womb-curled   knees touching
head   touching hands

beside her   on the plane
    warm bud
safe from   what shatters

your hands mine   on her small ones
    my face in   the dull
black pane   of the seat monitor

skin pale   breath ragged
    heart spinning   faster down
the runway   his words

fueling dread   as the plane lifts
    page after   burning page
fastened   to the turbulent

mind of what was   home
   to no home   a future
built on flame

Fire and Wine

To push away foundation rock,
mounds of pebbled glass hiss and click
around feet. Green, amber, clear
bottles shattered by flame, melted smooth,
as log upon log fell into the furnace.

A father's hoard for days' ends, the best saved
to celebrate, enrich a victory. Not a drop left
in this heap of what fed his cancer's pyre.

Mise en bouteille au château,
articulate vintages hauled across ocean,
a continent, to vaporize in midnight's fire
lighting the great live oaks whose branches
danced in billowing heat while beams collapsed.

Or did blood-red Bordeaux soak into cellar dirt,
sacrificed to the beast that breathed through flames,
engorging room after room?

To scoop a handful, glass beads rattle
like a throat choked on surfeit, sputter of voice
from a dream: *No love here no joy denied me
buried before birth.* A rod-pierced woman
bent over sink flooding cries of an infant ghost.

What root reared these dreams? To dare to ask one night,
dinner, friends in our old home. A fan blade snapped,
sailed over heads, cracked a mirror on the wall.

The House That Fire Built

What hungry ghost in need of a vessel,
of a man hollowed by his past, wounds licked raw,
preserved in alcohol, cauterized with meth,
his being swelling from pole to pole until reason
is a pool of oil, the blunt head of a match.

What hunger appeased at last by fire and wine
the ancients thought miracle enough
to salve the wound of any god?

Wine thought to lift to lips, sip blind
to the festering stock of inheritance. Now
a pile of pretty pebbles glistening in the sun.

Kirk Glaser

The Stranger

"Who's that?" asked from embers
as we dig through debris
in the foundation's pit.

A man swerves down the driveway,
stained jersey, cut-off jeans,
cap pulled low. "Who the hell?"

To pull our feet through
powdered ruin, to clamber
up concrete and stand on the road.
Coals clink quiet music
tuned to the sun's rising heat.

"Gabe?" "That's not him."
He stops at me, red face
bloated, slick with tears.

"Hey … Gabe?"
It's awful, I'm so sorry,
swaying, head down, twitching,
hand held out.

To take it—swollen, smooth,
weedy grip. His eyes flicker under
puffed lids, a shamed dog.

*The oily rags. The fire
marshal said he thinks*

The House That Fire Built

that's what happened.
One that could bite.

My car to his side, flame-shorn
of paint, metal warped by heat,
rims melted to a puddle.

"No water, no container
like the label tells you?"
To say it serves a hunger.
You exhale, descend back
to shifting blackened marble
chunks, sifting for jewelry
under a table's ghost.

Gabe jumps at a crunch of cinder,
click of a camera where the fire
inspector paces a black circle
etched in concrete, lens to eye.

Who's he? Head twitching
as he stares. *Why's he taking pictures?*
"Legarti, investigator
for the insurance company."

Why are you are here?
Why am I?
What do we hope to find?

Did he say anything?
About the rags or ... anything?
The day was so hot when I left,
but I didn't think they could—

"It's done, Gabe, an accident,
whatever happened," bitter on the tongue
for throwing him that bone.

Eyes on Legarti,
he touches blackened ribs,
a log wall speared against sky
by iron stakes, all that holds them
from the pit. Then walks away.

"What did he want?"
I shrug, rub soot from an eye
descending back
into the house of ash,

a home not three weeks,
no time to be more than a dream
of a hungry beast to crouch,
to hoard, to smolder in fury,

to wait for a hand to do as it bid.

Ground Vision

To sift through the fire's ruin
a hunger to hold
                       something spared
already a worn tooth in the mouth

To smother a heart with ash
                              breath
rough inside the stale fiber mask

To kneel in a pit cooling gray
and pull wire rims
                     from a mound
        of cinder and melted plastic

To hold a father's glasses
against blue sky   worn
       through a world war
                      fitted
                after his death
        to my vision

To be broken and soldered
        and broken
                and saved in a drawer
no longer a drawer

To slip them in a shirt pocket
sockets hollow
                temples twisted

Kirk Glaser

    To keep searching
        To forget
           until pricked in the chest
a small bloom of red
                    as the day sifts the body
through its loss

Wires Like Snakes

Alone, Legarti and crew gone to lunch,
    we prod and kick
        heaps of glass   burnt books
        fabric sodden in water and chemical foam.
Looking
        for what stays a fire's touch, a gem,
            a pack of photos   a journal
            in the center of a charred box
unscarred enough to think to keep.

                Feet crunch, a cough
from the far end of the pit. Gabe.

    Why is he still here?

I want to help.
    He climbs over a log, kicks
        at a pile of clothes.
You're such good people,
    why did this happen to you?
            Let me help.

He hoists, grunting   an iron sheet
    rust-stained black   wide and tall as a door.

"What's that?" I can't help ask.

    The back of your piano. Matter of fact.

Fire-sprung strings wind around pins,
        uncoiling now   snakes pulling skyward
the old upright's iron plate,
          a black door burning against blue sky.

He lets it drop.
          We jump back.
      A thump and hiss   it slides in soggy debris
close to where we stand.

"Listen, Gabe. You don't need to be here,
      you don't have to help." Careful
      what I say.

He stares where wires writhe,
turns up the driveway.

*

To dig under midsummer sun,
damp stench   charred wood, plastic
to fill our heads
          to dumbly obey
     the mind's need
    to stare into devastation
        to search   to behold
as if to make an order of things.
    The body's need
          to touch, to smell,
          to taste in the teeth,
          to sift until the stink

and sweat runs rivulets down sooty skin.

What to do but plunge
                fingers into
the fact of loss   everyone's inheritance,
      the terrible intimacy of ash.

My mother disappeared when I was twenty,
        a voice out of the blue-black afternoon.
        Gabe stands on a mound above us,
        red-faced, cap low.

"I thought he'd gone,"
        a chill down the limbs.

She met this guy and fell in love.
Took all her money out of the bank
and ran off with him.
                A wind kicks up,
            embers tick.
They caught him with the body
of a woman and linked him to deaths
of two others whose corpses they found.
He pulls at clumps of fabric
                clinging to hangers.
Not my mother's.
      Behind him   a red-tailed hawk
      spirals up currents
      over the charred field.

Kirk Glaser

The glare hurts eyes.   I stare down
over the mounds that were rooms.

He got everything and killed them.
He got everything she owned.

The inspector and his crew
            drive down   muscles release.

            Is that his final calculation?
                        Loss equates to loss   a life
                        reduced to things.
                        What chance cheats each of us
                                    from inheriting.

Gabe lifts a beam and shoves it aside
            stirring up
            a swath of embers
            squats   hand hovering

It's still warm underneath,
                        and looks at us.

Found

your hands dig   cinders under nails
marble shards   mark the spot

an heirloom box   stolen? did he?
sun beats   hours to nothing

found beyond   melted chains
a few stone beads   scattered pearls

when a spark glints   too sharp to be
confounded   with mere shimmer

of melted glass   carbon-scorched
facets unscathed   the wedding diamond

leaping to hand   grandmother's ring
shank and shoulder   melted to

rusting nails   the brilliant
home in your   cinder-creased palm

you never saw   the house burn
but keep hearing   glass crack

in dreams   you drew
a woman   skin shattering

her hands   cups of flame
oval diamond   falling into

Kirk Glaser

her palm   like a hope
too adamant   to burn

A Mother's Craft

Rhiannon curls in a corner—
our old home, her empty room.
No! Go away! when we reach for her.
The sting of words our daughter needs
to wrap around a sadness
she cannot name: Loss,

the halls we practice walking
all our lives. Well on her way
down the path—three years old,
her toys and books, her bed
swallowed by dragon flame,
and thrown back to a room
hollow to what made it home.

How to console her? Say
be thankful our bodies spared
fire's hungry magic? Words
to feed a mortal fear
still unkindled. Better to hold
that knowing a little longer.

You offer a hand. She crawls
behind the door, comes out
at the sound of crying,
climbs into mother's lap,
touching tears. "It hurts," you say,
arms curling around her. "It hurts."

Kirk Glaser

All together we cry, turning
to hugs, a song hummed,
a favorite story—
children tricked and stolen
into the cold ash forest
by Heckedy Peg who lost her leg
and will eat them up.

But their mother knew
her children's favorite things
and divined their joys to rescue them.
Devouring craft overpowered
by mother wit nursed on love.

Then breakfast, a new day,
one more away from fire.

The Altar Stones

What can't be   burned   still
prickling to find
                 fingers of quartz
black and red volcanic shards

plucked when I scraped
over Inyo desert
                 four days and nights
no food   a little water

to shed the boy seeded with fear
by father death
                 hunting a path
for the man   to go on from there.

Four days spent   tracing veins
earthquake thrust
                 minerals scattered like cones
under desert
             juniper   piñon

a few stones   to circle the body
through the hungering
                 nights to be   my east and west
my north   south   below and above

shards glinting starlight under
desert-fibered trees
                 whose roots sip
minerals ground by time

traced in water   trickling through sap
up to flicker
                in needle and bark
a thousand years or more

phantom quartz   etched spire
milky twin
                fire agate
black obsidian   all

for a spell to set my way
until buried here
                lost in a blaze
faint before fire that forges stone.

Fire Inspector

1. Incident Report

"I don't get it." He wipes sweat from his brow,
staring at the hull of the car, paces to charred logs
spiked and leaning over the concrete pad.
"How did the garage over here burn hot enough,"
walking back to me, "to ignite the car over here?"

I read for the nth time the tag on his black suit:

> Paul Legarti
> Pearce Fire Investigators

Hired by insurers to ... what, exactly?
"Wouldn't the tank explode from the heat?"

"Big fireball? Only in the movies."
He ducks his head inside the car
seared to steel, steering column,
metal coils the ghost of seats.

"So hot you can't even tell the make."
He runs his boot around a circle eaten in asphalt.
"A worker says he left a can of oily rags here."

"Gabe? He told you?"

Legarti shakes his head. "Fire marshal.
Said a guy showed up morning after to finish
the decks, worried some rags started the fire."

"In this heat, isn't that likely?"

Legarti shrugs, folds his arms.

August sun, stench of foam-soaked ruins,
ticking coals a hiss in my ears.
Fire shock flares into dark rooms of the skull:
a leather arm, a burning rod, meat on a hook.
"Then what did?"

Legarti kicks at the edge of the hole,
like a bird pecking where a worm disappeared,
searching what slipped away and left
behind scorched blacktop, burnt car, our lives.

"What did." A proposition, eyeing me
from face to hands, then back at his boot
grinding the black hole. Not a bird,
a man punishing the ground to release fire's jinn.
And what then?

2. Interrogation

Where were you both the night of the fire?

> Back East with our daughter,
> visiting my mother.

You came back when you heard about it?

The House That Fire Built

    We were on our way.

It happened the night before you *planned* to come home?

    What does that mean?

Any idea the cause?

    (A hungry ghost? A father's past?
    Do you think the same and hold your tongue?)

    Maybe wiring, the lights sometimes flickered.
    What about the rags?

And you lived here how long?

    Three weeks. The blunt fact
    cracking open husk of nightmare:
    burnt-hide beast scrabbling from cellar dirt, swelling
    into smoke, flame-tooth jaws to swallow
    furniture, clothes, walls, turns to us,
    Rhiannon pulled close in our arms.

Three weeks?

    Legarti's stone face splinters, surprise in his eyes
    and something else—sympathy? calculation?

Had you moved anything out?

What?

Antiques, paintings, anything?

No, we just moved in, most of it still in boxes. Why?

Who did you buy it from, any problems with the old owners?

We didn't buy it. My father lived here before dying
of cancer.

Other heirs?

No, well, my brother Ben, but he has a mental illness.
We're his trustees.

Did they get along?

He's schizophrenic, doesn't get along with himself,
but yes, well enough. What do my brothers
have to do with our house burning down?

Brothers? You only mentioned one.

Chris is dead. Not adding, *most likely*,
hearing at last the foolish candor kindled
by need to talk through shock.
But not with this man paid to get facts,
or twist them for insurers, find
someone to blame, deny a claim.

It'll take a few more days to inspect the site.
Will you be around if I have more questions?

    We can't seem to leave.
    Is it okay to dig through ... what's left?

It's your property.
Legarti, waving his hand, walks away.

3. *Illumination*

We watch him pace the foundation, stare
into the pit, before we say good morning.

"Can we talk?" Pulling out his pad and pen.
"You called us here."
Legarti's back to the morning sun,
the glare in our eyes, his face dark angles.
"Do you have any enemies?"

You reach a hand into air beside me,
fingers enfold fingers, a numb tingling.
"What are you talking about?"

"Anyone who might want to burn down the house,
get even with you, maybe your father.
Anyone angry or jealous about you inheriting all this."
His arm a black rod seared by sun sweeps the site.

All this. Dizzy, I stare at the house's pit.
      Mounds of metal, melted plastic,
          burnt boxes,
    our possessions on the pyre
    of your father's life.

"Enemies?" The word charring the tongue.
"No, no one. We're honest people. Wait,
are you saying someone—"

"I'm not saying anything. My job to cover
every angle. Did anyone have access to the house?"

"Just a friend, checking on the place. And Gabe.
He didn't have a key but came to oil the decks,
apparently, though we told him not to."

"The worker with his oily rag story?"

I nod. "He's the one who called me
about the fire, during a layover in Detroit."

"He had your cell?"

"No, one of those white courtesy phones."

Legarti gives me a deadpan look. "He called you
on an airport phone, to let you know?
Is this Gabe a friend?"

"No, someone the contractor hired."

"And he tracked you down. At an airport."

The words snake like embers through my veins.
"My mother told him our flights. He got her number."
Not till this moment wondering how.
"Didn't you talk to him yesterday?"

"He was here?" Legarti's eyes widen.
He scratches a dead pen against his pad, fumbles
in his pocket for another. "Why didn't you tell me?"

"Didn't your men see him jump our gate—
the one you padlocked, like we had to?"
Your words biting at how they barred us
from the house. "We didn't recognize him at first,
his face puffy, red, like he'd been crying."
"He walked right past you,
while you were taking pictures."

Legarti scribbles, curses under his breath.
"This guy, Gabe, I want to see him. Soon."

Timepiece

Where lie   the hands
a gear   a father's
          watch

the alligator skin   band darkened
by sweat   from long dead
          wrist

the twenty-one   minute jewels
glinted fire   now scattered in
          ash

held since   a teen when
I dragged my father   from shallows'
          water

pushed against   chest stars minutes
failed to   breathe back
          life

somewhere now   in ruin under foot
the two-inch square   of stainless
          steel

the casing   wedding date   initials
love inscribed   in time
          lost

Fingers of Flame

Alone with Legarti at the house's pit,
his face a silhouette, back against
morning sky: I want names,
everyone who could have been here.
Most don't know how fire flares.
I need to see hands, arms, faces
before burns heal, hair grows back.

The house's stink scrapes at my skull.
Dizzy, vision tunneling, seeking a face,
a name. Legarti black against blue sky,
a cutout shadow, eyes hunting mine.

*

That night, friends over for dinner,
arson parches our tongues, a word
to spit out as its fingers of flame
reach down the throat and grab the spine.

Telling them what we know
and don't. How Legarti walked us
through the house-no-house
pointing to flashpoints—
dark gasoline scar in the garage,
corner logs where fire flared
and climbed fresh oil, a blackened pit
where our bed had stood.

But who? why? they ask, we ask.
That's when the burnt fingers slip

loose their grip enough for us to see
and with the same breath say, Gabe.
Who tracked us down, who told his story
over an airport phone—driving up that morning,
feeling something bad. The house still
smoldering, the crews searching for bodies,
asking him was anyone home.
How he left oily rags, his fear,
an accident, an accident.

And again the day we saw him.
                We didn't know who was walking down the hill.
His mustache gone, a blue cap pulled low.
                No sideburns, no thick wavy hair.
His face was swollen and red and shiny.
                I thought from sweat and crying.
He held out his hand, smooth, puffy, hairless.
                No day labor hand.
Telling his story again and again.
                Adding his work clothes burned up, too.
Wait, says a friend, his clothes?
That's what I asked.

Yeah, they were a mess
so I used them to wipe up the decks,
no good anymore, I stuffed them
in a can to get rid of later.

It made no sense, so much happening, I forgot
until now—clothes splattered with oil, caught in fire's claws.

      Torn off in panic, evidence to destroy.
Then later that day.
     The strangest story.
We had no idea why.

  My mother ran off with this guy,
  took all her savings. Later
  they caught him with bodies
  of two women, not my mother's.
  She was never found.

We didn't know.
     We were in shock.
We didn't know.
    The things he said.
    What to look for.

And we let him go.

Night Ploy

Set the wire
    to trip a foot
pulled taut across
    the walk and door
Slip into bed
    touch hammer's shaft
set to seize from
    bedside floor

But no sleep will come
    no sleep will come
now that I know
    hands harbor flame
now that I know
    what he's done

Step outside
    under midnight stars
dense summer air
    a throbbing drum
What would he do
    if accused
if he knows we know
    what he's done

On the mountain road
    above the house
rhomboids of light
    twist over trees

The House That Fire Built

a pickup slows
    kills its lights
Under engine thrum
    a door squeaks wide
and feet scrape ground
    Does he stand there
peering down

A voice calls once
    twice—my name
or cricket song
    warped by internal
combustion rumble
    blood pounding ears
The truck door slams
    the engine guns
wheels spit gravel
    and burn in fear
the heart knowing
    what he's done

Leave It Alone

One of Everything

We freeze under fluorescent lights
dangling on silver chains,
rows of tubular suns coldly aligned

over aisles of drugstore goods.
"Can I help you?" a red-shirted girl asks,
silver ball bobbing on pierced tongue.

"We need one of everything." The girl
narrows her eyes. "I'm sorry?" "Not everything,
we have a toothbrush, just everything else."

The fire has glazed our humor like this,
pigment too dark for a high school girl
just saving up for her next tattoo.

Maybe she thinks we are among those
who rise from the river banks
each morning, crazy, lost, or damned

unlucky, wandering in for bandages,
juice, a jug of wine, alcohol wipes
to clean a needle and face another day.

"It's okay, we'll find what we need."
The girl walks away, leaving the question,
what do we need? Two minds pull me.

One set to fill our home again
with the myriad things that anchor a life.
The other on scent of a path burned clean,

tracking Muir through the Sierra range,
a crust of bread in his pocket,
cut fir boughs for a bed.

Or Bashō leaning on the staff of an ancient,
leaving his ramshackle hut by the river to gather
emptiness over a thousand leagues.

The Crone

No seed to sleep can sow itself,
no dream-root in these furrows
where halfway facts churned
over and over surface nothing but

What caused this? Fevered mantra
striking blades of thought
until at last darkness, sleep,
a dream before dawn:

I stand beside you,
my mother, and the dead—
father, grandparents,
your mother, your father
covered in mud at her feet.

The house built of flame
flickers around us. I reach
for the cellar door where your father
stored his wine, where dank breath
seeped through cracks. It crumbles

embers at my touch.
A crone breaks the frame,
massive as a cliff, wrapped in mineral cloaks,
her face crevices laced with iron and jade,
lips of mossy agate. She shrugs the house
of fire like dust from her shoulders,

stares with blank quartz eyes,
poised as if to crush us all.
> *I know your desire.*
> *It means nothing.*
> *I will capture the creature.*

Stone arms crack and boom,
mountains thrust skyward.
She spins, gypsum choking air
as she burrows too deep for the mind
to follow, emerges grasping an oily mass,
charred, leathery, writhing absence of light
caught in the rock folds of her robes.

Awake in the gray dawn, I grasp
for what was snagged in the dream,
but the shape, knowing, slips itself from mind
like a worm beneath upturned rock.

I lie in bed, willing the dream's return:
rock-earth crone swallowed the creature—no,
entombed it between plates on her back,
a carapace of obsidian.

Wriggling limbs, knotted hands
caught in the seam of her shell
desperately pulling at light.

The House That Fire Built

The crone spoke:
> *An irritant, hungry, so many,*
> *impelled to do what it did.*
> *Now sealed, to be consumed.*

Cliffs eaten by wind, coastlines sinking
under sea, islands that rise and slam into shore,
the slow passage of devouring Earth.

I drift back toward sleep and ask:
What is this world? Who are you?
That thing you pulled from under the house,
what did it need to do? Why?

But the crone dwells deeper than dream,
too fierce to call forth, a voice distilled in fog,
words broken over a dark sea:

> *Leave it alone.*

Leave It Alone

The adjuster sends a letter
Accusation
                Arson
Insurant paid Subject
                to set the Flame

A demand   Present Suspect
           Gabriel J———
      as if ours to conjure

But he's vanished   voicemail full
Housemate shrugs
      filling the door
           Left without a word

So we call the sheriff

*

Driveway asphalt   soft underfoot
      in afternoon heat   we stand
with the deputy
          stiff Kevlar man
under tan uniform

We repeat the story
      told so often   dull edged
though words still cut   bluntly yours
      honing themselves   against mine

The House That Fire Built

The deputy stares past us
    at the foundation pit
still ticking under hot sun   still stinking
synthetic odor   the modern burn
    toxic scar on the land

"Arson's hard to prove   too much
    time   burns heal"
A sunglassed glare
    "Anything missing?"

You smirk   "Kind of hard to tell"
    "No bike frames   chain saw
no metal in the ashes"

"Stolen goods   best chance to catch him"

"So we file for robbery
    not arson?"

His arms creak   crossing them
    in the heat
"Have to find the goods   and reason
    to believe he took them
Best bet   track him down
    get his address   vehicle information"

"What?"   "You want *us* to find him?"
    "Isn't that your job?"

A grimace   a sigh
    he kicks the asphalt
stares past us

"My advice?   Arsonists hold grudges
    get revenge
        even go after judges
You're better off
        to leave it alone"

Words like claws   I want to curse
    his thick-shelled advice
        but my throat grows tight
the phrase clambering
    through the crone's mouth

Fire Insurance

Summoned to a strip mall, a door whose corporate
name through concrete amnesia feigns to elicit

nostalgia for farmers who tilled the good lands
(once Missions yoked to god and plow Ohlone hands).

Inside sits the thin man, shaved head, no smile,
who calls us by surname, no Mr. or Ms., blunt guile

of a gym coach or ex-cop. He presses *Play*
on the small black box, commences to flay

us with questions: *You let strangers known
only a few months have access to your home?*

The gears lurch into motion, a machine
policy oiled to grind us up between

fiscal cycles, our loss meaningless
against a ledger's drop in interest.

When our turn: Gabe, will you tell us what he said?
Confidential. What? Does that mean he confessed?

Not in company interest to pursue, nothing to glean
from him, no accounts, no property to impose a lien.

The thin man who slices at our loss with fear:
Expect a report in the mail. Depending, you'll hear

from one of our teams—an agent, or lawyer.
So into the hot asphalt wind we wander,

spun upside down, wondering how deep this will blow,
or the nadir reached, we turn to flee the inferno.

Telephone Call

They asked if you paid me to do it.
Is it true, they really think someone
burned down your house?

>Your ear by mine, you whisper,
>"Don't let him know we know. They promised
>not to tell him we were told."

"What? That's crazy, Gabe.
It's about the claim,
intimidate you, find someone
to blame, make them pay."

They asked if I saw things
leave the house, if you owed me
money, treated me bad. If you
asked me to do it. If I did.

>Worth nothing to them,
>save what threats can breed—
>scare him into confession, say we paid him
>to burn our home, his get out of jail card free.

I told them no, you're the best.
Are they waiting for tests?
If it was the rags, can they
put me in jail? Take my truck?
Did they accuse you, too?

> Accuse, accuse. Voice on a phone
> near or far? What brought him to us?
> What would he do to save himself?

"They don't know the cause, Gabe,
just groping for excuses not to pay us.
They'll give up soon. Look, I need to go."

*Okay but I wondered can you
pay me what you owe me.*

"Owe you?"

For oiling the decks.

"You mean the ones that burned all night?"

> You touch my arm: "Pay him, let it go."
> Phone against chest, I mouth No.
> You look to our daughter playing on the floor.
> "Is that a risk you want to take?"

"Sure, Gabe, how many hours,
what do we owe?"

> How many hours, how many days
> while we were gone, imagining our home his
> before he oiled carpets, clothes, our bed,
> and struck a match at the end of a stifling day?

The House That Fire Built

Um, around twenty-two, call it twenty,
that'll do. I know you guys
have been through a lot.

"I'll mail you a check. Where are you?"

Well, I'm leaving town. Could we meet?

"Meet you?"

> My heart beats hard. You nod. "A chance
> to find out where he's going, tell the sheriff."
> But how to face him, knowing what I know.

"Okay, Gabe, how's tomorrow, noon?"

Your place? The one you moved from
before ... um ... is that where you are?

"No, let's meet at the coffee shop,
the one on Highway 9."

> Away from our home, keep him away,
> drugged-out manikin of a hungry ghost
> that lured us into the burning lair.
> Now a game of guile, masked innocence:
> second chance to look for burns, singed hair,
> take photos of his truck, question him,
> see if he trips up, phone recording under shirt.

Kirk Glaser

A Reckoning

Slapping oil on decks, head throbbing from the stench and heat, the beers he's been drinking since noon, Gabe drops the brush and glares at the bay glimmering under late sun.

No more nights sleeping on the deck, Gabe-Gabe. They come back tomorrow. No more watching the stars a sky full of embers just for you. He tries to ignore the voice, new one that started when working here, that creaks a leather arm around his shoulders, holds tight, rasps through cinder-dry lips in his ear.

No more Indians on the cliff, Gabe-Gabe, calling to you, his chin pushed up to look. You belong here, they said so, not those fuckers who call it their home. He piles cans and oily rags on a tarp, tamps down lids to still the voice. Time to go.

No more good life when they return. No longer his, the vaulted ceilings, the windows facing the bay, the antiques and piano, the paintings and clothes and big TV.

All they inherited, and what did you get, Gabe-Gabe. Your mother's money some bastard's who killed her, spent on the fucker's lawyers, mouth crackling in his ear. *Murdered, and you couldn't prove a thing. Your mother's life you fucking failed. Even the money they pay you, Gabe-Gabe, not yours—two months rent, the meth to keep you going grunt grunt. You owe it all. None of it's yours.*

He smacks his brush against a bench, oil splattering sunlight. *There's cash stashed someplace, Gabe-Gabe, jewelry. Break a window, they'll think they were robbed. Take it, they'll never blame you.*

Searching the bedroom when a car noses down the road. *Bitch they have watching the place. Didn't trust you, Gabe-Gabe?* He runs outside, grabs a brush. Under the deck oiling a post, muttering. Her eyes narrow. "What are you doing here?" Hugs herself, looks around. "Is there someone else?"

Bitch. What's wrong, can't come up with a story? "Nobody, just me, they called and asked me to finish oiling the decks before they came home." She stares at him. *Grab her, no one will know.* Leathery hand rubbing his crotch. He swats it away, keeps his other painting the post, delicate as stroking a woman's leg. "It's late, you should go." Fear in her eyes. *Knock her down, take her.* "Just finishing." She closes the door, he hears it lock.

After she leaves he kicks it in, hunts the house, dumps drawers, pulls boxes and clothes from closets, flips mattresses, swears. No cash. A cigarette he dropped smolders on the floor, a foot crushing it into the wood. *Thought they were so generous when your truck broke down, feeding you dinner, taking you home. Poor Gabe-Gabe, needing handouts. Fuck them, fuck this house.*

He grabs a jewelry box, staggers down the hall, slamming
   walls. Opens another beer, lights a joint, sits at the
   kitchen counter. All over the floor the crap he's spilled,
   broken plates, furniture knocked over. *You'll never make
   it look right. They'll know it was you, Gabe-Gabe. Better
   make sure they never do. You know how, you've known all
   along what it was coming to.*

Hand lighting a cigarette, another pushing him to the garage.
   Eyes glassy and twitching like after a night of booze and
   speed, fingers trembling over the gas can. *Five gallons,
   that fucker so prepared. Cleared the field on his shiny new
   mower to keep fire from their new home. Needed you on
   back, though, when wheels spun. Should have let you mow,
   you could've jockeyed it all alone. You could have jockeyed
   her, Gabe-Gabe, when he wasn't here. But you blew it,
   coward, like always, fear juicing your bone.*

Can splashing on the rugs wrapped up in the garage, on boxes
   still unpacked. Lugged through the house, spilling gas on
   floors, walls, the mess he's made, slowing to pool it on his
   desk, her dresser, their bed.

*More oil in the garage, Gabe-Gabe. Two weeks slapping these
   decks for them in the hot sun while they're off having fun.
   The decks will go up fast, but the garage is dry, and his car
   so close, might end up spilling some.*

Not sure how a maul slid into his hands, windshield smashed,
   oil flung inside. *No justice in the world, Gabe-Gabe, not for*

you, not your mother. Make it even. Just a match to light up the big scene.

He backs away, looking to his truck up the hill. *Do it.* Stench of gas spinning his head, sweat-soaked shirt clinging to skin. *Do it!* A sudden wind, the door to the house flying wide. *Prove for once you're a man, not some pussy walking dead.*

Flames explode from the garage, knock him down. He's never lit one this big. Hair singes on head and arms, heat burrowing into skin like worms eating him alive. *Feel it rise, Gabe-Gabe. Feed it more.* Eyes burning in his skull, he fumbles with the door into the house. A hand throws his cigarette down the hall, fire snaking from one pile to the next following his path to their bedroom. He stumbles up the driveway, coughing and shaking.

Sun down, sky darkening, the massive oaks over the house flickering with flame. *Come back inside, Gabe-Gabe. Feel it burn.* No. The voice, not him to blame.

He stinks of oil and smoke, skin raw from the explosion. He touches his face, mustache burnt to stubble, eyebrows gone, arms black. No. Leave before someone sees flames lighting the sky. He clambers into his truck, a hand pulling on his back.

Your dream house flying into the night, Gabe-Gabe. Don't you want to be with it? Make yourself at home, feel the flame.

No? Fine. Get lost, then. Poor Gabe-Gabe, no one cares about you. This house was never yours. You were mine.

Now watch me rise.

The Café of Lost Confessions

An hour early, sleepless, no sign of his beat-up Chevy,
nightmare circling the streets of the mountain town
waiting for the man who turned us to cinder.

"Let's just say, 'Why did you do it, Gabe?'
Catch him off guard." I want to accuse, accuse,
let him know what I know. You squint in morning sun,
squeeze out words: "He burned down our house
after sharing a meal. What else could he do?
Let him think we're friends, pay him. Spirit him far away."
"But if he confessed, we'd have it on our phones."
"I want to know, too. The worst is not knowing.
But who would stop him coming after us—
the sheriff, whose job we're doing?"

We stop, his gray truck beside the café.
A dizzy clarity in the heat, sunlight
crazed through rustling leaves.
We reach for each other's hand. "Where is he?"
"There." Gabe hunched at a table outside.
We pass the truck, my phone low, clicking
plate under dented front, side of the bed
pocked with buckshot and paint peeling,
bubbled as if from heat.

"Slumped like he's going to fall off the chair."
"Is he asleep?" "Or on something."
"Hey Gabe," you call at his back,
small pleasure when he jumps.
"Oh, it's you guys. Hi." Eyes dark

bags, face puffy like the day
he staggered down the driveway.

"How are you doing, Gabe?" Casual as
you can be. We sit. Gabe shakes his head.
"That insurance guy, what a bastard,
like a cop. Asked me the same questions over
and over, like trying to trip me up."
He fidgets with a bottle cap. "Took pictures
of my hands and face, even my ears."
Two weeks since the fire. Hat pulled low over
uneven hair, mustache and sideburns growing back,
red spots on wrists, long sleeves despite the heat.
"Then he asked if I did it, just like that,
if you paid me to burn down your house."
He shakes his head. "Can you believe it?"

"What did you say, Gabe?" He won't look up.
"I told him no. Then he asked if I saw you guys
moving stuff out. I laughed, said I just helped
move everything in. *They're good people,*
I told him." Gabe sighs, sinks in his chair.
"I told him you helped me when my truck was dead."
Eyes filling with tears, an ache in his voice.
"I left the day after I saw you. Drove up to Stockton.
I couldn't sleep, cried all the time."

Your hand over mine. Let him talk, see what spills.
"I kept thinking about you guys and your little girl.
You don't deserve this, and right after your dad died.

THE HOUSE THAT FIRE BUILT

I felt awful, kept thinking it must be my fault.
I drove into the mountains to drive my truck off a cliff,
chickened out. What good would it do?"

Suicide? We dart eyes, ice blade in my gut.
Why tell us? Guilt? A plea? A hook
for sympathy, a way to set himself free?
Another icy blade, shame, the wish
his foot stayed on the gas.

Gabe looks up. "Will you tell me, when they find out?
Even if it was the rags, I want to know."
"They're treating us the same," you say, leaning in,
confiding, lesson learned from con-artist father.
"They want bank records, invoice for a moving truck,
even boarding passes to prove we left."
"Those bastards," Gabe says, "Big company,
all that money, and won't give you a penny."
"We're not worried, Gabe, we have nothing to hide."
My one jab. Gabe shifts as if to wriggle free.

We ask what he'll do next, try to learn where
he's going. Off to play ball for a month, a league
in the Valley. Try to forget, get on with life.
And then you ask, "So what do you think started it,
Gabe? In your heart. What's your gut feeling?"
Eyelids quiver, half close, shut.
His shoulder twitches, head jerks to the side
like somebody slamming it over and over.
"I ... I ... I...," voice a soul-deep ache,

as if someone else tries to break through.
Hands tremble on the table, bottle cap pinched,
twisting and twisting. "I ... don't ... I don't ..."
Gabe's head jerks, eyes open, close,
roll up in the sockets. Lips tight, twisting
as if pried to form words wanting, not wanting,
to reach the world. Say it, Gabe, say it.
And then what would we do?
"I don't know." Eyes open, head drops.
"I'm afraid it's something I did."

As close as he'll come.

"So, you can pay me for the work?"
You pull out the checkbook and smile.
"You mean for oiling the deck that's now toast?"
He looks down, fingers pressed white against the blue cap.
I grimace, wishing the line had been mine.
"But you wanted cash, right, Gabe?" I play the card.
He nods. "Yeah, I don't have a bank account,
and I'm collecting unemployment. Cash is better."
"You didn't tell me, Kirk. I brought the checkbook."
"Can't you get cash from the ATM?"
You shake your head. "Not enough in my account."
A posed frown, as if figuring out what to do.
"You could write a check to Gabe, deposit it,
and withdraw the cash." "I guess so."
"But Gabe, you need to sign it. And probably
your driver's license, to make sure it clears."
Would he suspect the scheme to get his ID?

The House That Fire Built

"So then you can do cash?"
He pulls out his wallet, Nevada license.
You steady your hands to write the check,
slide it to him. He signs his name in a jittery script.

Gabe writes on a napkin how to be reached,
slow, like a first grader practicing to write.
After you put the bills in front of him,
he pushes the napkin toward me, pulls in the pile,
like a card player with a winning hand.
"I feel better, talking with you guys." A smile
as he counts, shoulders widening,
a bird ready to take flight. He leans back,
sun catching his face as his head tilts up.
Under his cap bare patches on eyebrows
darkened with pencil, rough rows of lashes.
My gut grows cold.

We stand, Gabe reaches a hand to me.
I shake it. He heads to his truck.
We sigh, then laugh, then laugh again
how we mirror each other. "Coffee?"
You nod. "He didn't shake my hand."
"I need to wash mine."

Inside, a weight on my shoulder, I jump.
Gabe's hand. "I just had to come back and
make sure, no hard feelings, right?"
I smile. "No hard feelings, Gabe."
He squeezes my shoulder, a poison

trickles through me. You catch my eye,
holding your breath and I hear:
Let him go, just let him go.
Gabe turns and saunters out.

"No hard feelings," you say, a bitter smirk.
"I almost lost it." My hand shaking
as I pick up my drink.
"He's feeling good. We're his pals,
doesn't think we suspect a thing."
"Thank god," I say.
"Oh now you're happy we didn't let on?"
I shrug. "He almost confessed."
"Did you see his eyebrows, the pencil liner?"
I nod, blow on my coffee. "He's free."

The Angels and Devas Debate Karmic Parameters in the Cloudy World of Mortals

> *Gabriel: Our father noted my one nature, destruction, & said:*
> *'Go forth as fire in all its forms. It will be an abused nature,*
> *yet attend it.'*
> *And so I cleanse too, & I illuminate reflection.*
>   —adapted from* The Changing Light at Sandover,* James Merrill

Miyka'el: Our Query, today, fellow messengers:
Can causes and conditions haunt a home?

Mara: What, the past pervade a place?
Even as it haunts these cauldrons of thirsty flesh
half blind (at best) to behavior's consequence?

Uriel: And why not? Just as their despair
over what has been, their fear or longing
for what may or will never be
construct the frame of self
to shape a destiny, so too human action,
causation's dust, may infect a habitation.

Yama: Agreed, a house can be a heart
where a life leaves its karmic mark.
Oh, house builder, you implicate the unsuspecting,
hopes driven by fears and fears by hopes,
along the mundane path of life
caught in routine of being strung to things.

Azrael: Then what of the future?
May it, too, inhabit a place? Exhibit:
A woman crying to herself through the night

after she moves her family into the house
she dreamed into being, beams still bleeding
sap over children silent in their sleep,
where soon she will weep for a husband found
by her son face down at the bottom of the pool.

Mara: When will you let that one be?
You did your fool best warning them.
Perhaps too subtle with erratic chiming
from the old French clock—they failed to decrypt
that code. But please, a blunt message when
you dropped the father through rotten ice,
that pond's black mouth warning of water's menace.
So the son arrived here with drowned memories
to be seared by a house caught in another
father's blood and flame, hardly your fault.

Miyka'el: Back to our thesis, please.
Their future, thus, is merely past extrapolated.
Rarely may one of their hearts touch
the thread that leads into a storm
and be aware to pluck it short—

Mara: —as their bodies walk dumbly forward.

Uriel: No more possible, then, to be rescued
from a future, so many threads of past
approaching the needle's eye—specimen:
the man who smolders over murder
of a mother, drug-addled, strung to the hungry

ghosts woven by violence into the land,
lured by a father whose dead family
lay twisted in his hands.

Azrael: And before him, spirits, first humans
who tread lightly through redwood and oak,
all cut down by those who ignored the pattern
weft by sunlight and rain, warp of tremor and slide,
who rent the land first for fire and lime
to build cities, then again by heedless plan,
a house, its walls stained by unsettled death.

Yama: They culled the wounded man
with oil-soaked hands ready to do a fiery bidding.

Gabriel: Or might some angel, fierce
yet full of mercy, have thrust him
into the path to sear a redder cord than fire
that the house's hungers stretched
neck high across the threshold
to sever joy from the new family.

Angels in Chorus: What, he was your doing, then?

Miyka'el: Deftly done—they will never guess
you saved them by flame, will have to suffer
through to their own illumination.

Mara: Gabriel, you clever devil, you!

Inheritance of Fire

Song in Cinders

Say the house is a night we inherit,
and from a bed on a far shore we hear
fire rip through air, its twirls and licks
singing of sudden erratic deaths
as it lifts oil-soaked sheets to the sky.

Say from so far, the music lulls us to sleep,
and we dream of rooms filled with honey,
pushing through the thick amber heat
to lift our daughter in our arms so she may
grasp the leaf-lit tree and climb free.

Our lips split calling each other, *Where are you?*
but sweet flame cleaves our tongues
to the mouth's vault, and the unutterable
promises of daylight melt in our throats
smothering names love wicks from the heart.

Say we wake from the dream to enter
its ruins smoking on the dawn hillside,
shards of glass warm as skin, water
foaming among the music of cinders,
the *tink tink tunk* of a galaxy expiring in ash.

Names come now, each other's to walk beside,
our daughter's we call with scorched throats
to bear the future. Our hands scatter seeds
in the burnt field, cracked free by resins
awaiting flame, softened by breath
to release fire-wrought flowers, a blaze of grass.

Kirk Glaser

Swailing Field

Lying on a futon
in our old home
empty, burnt-out

end of another day
in summer heat,
our daughter asleep.

We turn to each other,
crickets singing,
hand finding hand

under borrowed sheets
and laugh in the dark
on the back-burned field of loss.

Why this giddy release?
It's gone, the dream is burnt.
The words like laughter

not what we imagined.
We're free. A seed cracked open,
its radicle delving our hearts.

All gone, ashes
spun skyward
from shattered urns—

father's, grandmother's
by angel or demon flame
prescribed to clear the field,

leaving us home,
flickering peace kindling
under heart's heaviness.

The Live Oaks' Fire Song

After rains
    another spring
we sprout   green
    from black-
  ened branches   leaves soon
to blanket
    charred earth
where the house stood

fire-scar   chevrons
    branding limbs   thick-barked
indifference   to flames
    that licked us   clean
  leaf tongues
    lighting the sky

we stretch   and sway
  in easeful generation

the blaze
    could not touch
  our canopy of roots
  locked into earth   rock
    gathering
mineral light   sipping
    beds of water
scarcely aware
  the upper world   disrupted

THE HOUSE THAT FIRE BUILT

save for a need
   to feed our
          skyward selves

Kirk Glaser

Inheritance of Fire

A father died
the house remained
beneath it   currents of a life
ate at foundation

Dry wind carving   bone canyon
whipping shed skin
rock teeth   grinding delusion
into hairline cracks
spreading   unseen
beneath our feet

How many times
you said   I want to pile
his possessions in the field
and burn them

Premonition   or desire
to turn bitter remnants
of him   to fuel
a back burn
to create a swailing line
to halt   darker inheritance

Or the need to be
burned clean to the bone

Only after winds
blew coals to black   and the rains
washed cinder into earth

THE HOUSE THAT FIRE BUILT

to see   to grasp
to inherit is to enter the cracks
in the bone   take the splintering
wind in the teeth   wear the dead
skin clinging to gold

Irritant in the Solution

Falling asleep   the slip past
another day walled
in fire's husk
        a question floats
why believe   a life any more
than a shining pebble
    batted about the sea?

A pearl   ill-formed   luminous
knocks against tidal cliffs
of the brain's vault
        pale glow   in night ocean
drifting behind eyes

It batters against
smooth walls   clamped shut
        the inner surface
of the self   rough shell
   locked to rougher shoals

Let go and drift
   through dream   time
tap against   another life
        dare to crack
open and swell   flesh
       to taste   salt-sweet
flesh   pearls spilling
from adjacent beds
        into the current

The House That Fire Built

no choice   but trust and love
    no joy
but to share all that time
will carry away

The pearl that endures
flesh and shell   born of irritant
    made into shining
seed carried   life to life
    the chance
      to be perfected again

When the land   breathes fire
    ocean tides tug
  the pearl
homeward

A Leaf of Ash

deep in the woods: gray-white
paper holding a specter of ink,
hand-scribed black against gray
against yellow madrone leaves
where it has settled

brittle, broken, and gone.

The log walls stood the night
spiked together, oil-soaked pine
crackling into flames eighty feet high
licking oak branches that danced with light
as they writhed over the roof-beams
before those collapsed, the household
of goods melting, shattering, charging the air
into a vortex of heat and smoke—
wind that billowed paper ash
over treetops, under the stars.

Brittle, broken, and gone

what floated past all reason of flame?
A letter or journal scrap, a child's drawing
to settle here by a redwood circle,
hundred-year-old children of ones lost
to sweat and axe and the dream
of wealth, cut to burn limestone to dust,
hauled down these mountainsides
for concrete that lifted the walls
of coastal cities.

The House That Fire Built

Brittle, broken, and gone

indecipherable ash rocking in the palm,
a morning, mid-wood breeze
as the August day grows hot and dry,
leaves ticking, the forest floor waiting
for its own fire to clear detritus of years,
feed soil, crack seeds to germinate, scar
the great trees who know how to stand above it,
take the black sear up their trunks,
the char that opens them to the pith,
and rise cell upon cell sunward
a thousand years or more.

Kirk Glaser

Fire's Way

The forest knows
           flames come
loss a moment suffering
      so that, *say it*,
new life grows.

Too long suppressed
        fire feeds
on dead limbs' pyres
            climbs high
into the canopy
threatening root to crown.

Or clears a field
           to open
a way past
       charred roof beams,
books, burnt rags   and bone
           china, the brittle
condition of things,
      into forest
where pyriscent seeds
            cracked by flame
    lick carbon
       with translucent roots,
tease nitrogen into leaves
             from deadwood and duff.

Fire casts light
     through wood and coal

The House That Fire Built

        and oil and atoms
    and yes lives
burning what clings
    to the mind's understory,
    clutters the dusty
        storehouse of the heart.

Controlled
        not to be
controlled.   Fire
    the two-faced god—
bone destroyer
        quickening spark
shadow caster
    star-bed piercing the night.

Kirk Glaser

The House That Fire Built

Trucks and excavator gone,
blackened earth pockmarks the field
dripping green in a cold rain,

bird song piercing the dense day's end.
Scarred foundation swept clean,
we walk the perimeter of a bad dream

and look with two minds: owners
inspecting work before writing a check,
a couple prodding at burnt strand ends

that entangled us in your father's past.
We never found his urn
or his father's or mother's—

fire cracked their clay, ashes spun
skyward on a swell of flame
or scraped up to be dumped

inland on ancient ocean bottom
where toxins leak from debris of home
after home as fires season this land.

Over the concrete rim and down,
we take in what remains, the almost nothing
but light scattered by shards of glass

piercing a carbon skin. Where my desk
stood mere weeks, the corner
of a book sucked down by muddy ash

catches my boot, hardcover binding erased
by fire, water, earth. I peel apart pulp
glued by rain and read to you

from a flame-chewed page, words burnt
brown in relief, eaten to smoke
as the page tapers to black end:

> You have to know when to let the old life go, take ...
> ... not look back and have regrets, I always
> say. Otherwise you will always be sad, because ...
> ... always losing something. That's the way life ...
> ... if you let misfortunes strike you too har ...
> ... won't see the new chance coming. If ...
> ... idn't know this I would not ...

In the shimmering dirt, in the clouds
dropping their semaphores of mist, is it
a cosmic joke framed as coincidence

or intractable truth left to flit meaning
behind the blunt rock of diurnal thought.
I peel another soggy page, rotten skin of fruit.

> ... didn't come true as we hoped ...
> ...sad when the old man died, even ...

... expecting it and hoping for it, that was natural...
...smell was the first sign. And then he didn't talk...
   ...then took to his bed and at the end begg...
     ...to be taken...
        ...his fine house, full of rich furniture...

The pages fall. A bitter laugh. Yours? Mine?
Inherited by fire, let it be, a father's story,
a mother's antiques, parents' urns, all our things,

the house riding the sky above the bay,
the spell it held us in, dreaming a home
forged free of the stories colliding there.

Let be the demon fire that saved us from a future
shadowed in nightmare. A house in the mind,
a house no longer here, the house that fire built.

We turn and walk up the hill.
You take my hand, a taste of ash
on the tongue, our bodies blown on the wind.

Notes

"Clearing the Field": two lines early on from Robert Frost's "The Tuft of Flowers."

"The Angels and Devas Debate Karmic Parameters in the Cloudy World of Mortals": Miyka'el, Uriel, Gabriel, and Azrael are angels referenced in Judeo-Christian, Islamic, and other scriptures and religious texts. The first three are often archangels who guard God's throne and the four primary directions (along with Raphael). Mara and Yama are from Buddhism/Hinduism, where devas are similar to angels (devas being celestial beings with godlike characteristics), though Mara is in a class of his own, technically not a deva. The following definitions are not complete (how could they be for such beings?) but point to their roles in the poem, here in order of appearance:

> Miyka'el: "Who is like God" (often as a question). Also Michael. In the Kabbalah, one of the four primary archangels, often considered the primary archangel, called on for protection, defender of the holy and good.
>
> Mara: A demon god in Hinduism and Buddhism of sensual desire, craving for earthly things, discontent, doubt, restlessness ... perhaps the ego personified. Mara is also often associated with death (or fear of it). He appeared to the Buddha at many points to try to lure him away from the path of enlightenment with the promise of sensual pleasures and wealth as well as fear of suffering and death.
>
> Uriel: "God is my flame." Often an angel of repentance and salvation.
>
> Yama: Generally a deity of death and justice. One of the twelve devas in some Buddhist systems.

Azrael: "The one whom God helps." A benevolent angel of death who helps transport souls after they die. More prevalent in Islamic and Christian traditions than Judaism.

Gabriel: "Man of God." Gabriel communicates God's will to humanity (to prophets such as Daniel); in James Merrill's *The Changing Light at Sandover*, Gabriel is associated with fire as destroyer/cleanser/enlightener.

"Fire's Way": Italicized lines from James Merrill, *The Changing Light at Sandover*

Acknowledgments

This book would not exist without the love, creativity, and support of Miranda and Rhiannon Janeschild, who lived through these events with me. Thank you, Miranda, for trusting me to tell parts of your story, deepening my understandings, and spending so many hours and years talking about the poems and the events, reliving traumas, uncovering new insights, and healing and growing together. Rhiannon, you were three years old when these flames and hungry ghosts swirled around our family. We protected you from them as much as possible, so to have you read the manuscript as an adult, live the experience anew, and create works of art using oils, paper, fire, and water inspired by these poems has been profoundly moving. For your cover art to embrace this book feels like a completion to this mythic journey of our family. A special and bittersweet thank you to "Do" Roberts, who did not live to see this book published but nurtured and shaped it uniquely as mother and fellow poet.

I also wish to acknowledge with deep gratitude those who read the manuscript at various stages of its long gestation. First, profound thanks to Juan Velasco-Moreno, who cared for this book as if it were his own, reading multiple versions and offering tremendous insights. Your belief in these poems and the story's importance helped me through many times of doubt and frustration. I also wish to thank April Ossmann for her enthusiasm about this project early on and offering critical editing help, as well as to John Sibley Williams, Miah Jeffra, Claudia McIsaac, and Tim Myers for valuable feedback to rethink poems and the manuscript's flow. Thanks to Elsewhere Studios, in particular Henry Kunkel and Carolina Porras, for providing the time and space to delve deeply into reworking and assembling the book, and to Community of Writers, where a number of these poems were born. And the deepest thanks to Marc Vincenz and MadHat Press for the faith and energies to make this book a reality.

Thank you to the editors of the journals who published versions of the following poems:

"A Leaf of Ash," *Catamaran Literary Reader*

"A Reckoning," published as "Dream House," *Third Street Review*

"Clearing the Field," "White Courtesy Telephone," *Ginosko Literary Journal*

"Cremation," "Under Currents," *spoKe*

"Fire and Wine," *The American Journal of Poetry*

"First Loss," *Rockvale Review*

"Found," *Chicago Quarterly Review*

"I Breathe," *Steam Ticket*

"Indian Cove" and "What's Left on the Tongue," *Nimrod International Journal*

"Inheritance of Fire," *Marsh Hawk Review*

"One of Everything," *Gold Man Review*

"Song in Cinders," *Literary Laundry*

"The Crossing, III," *Santa Clara Review*

"The Live Oaks' Fire Song," *Osiris*

About the Author

KIRK GLASER is a poet and fiction writer whose work has been nominated twice for the Pushcart Prize and has appeared in *The Threepenny Review, Nimrod, Chicago Quarterly Review, Catamaran, The Cortland Review, The San Francisco Chronicle*, and elsewhere. Awards for his work include an American Academy of Poets prize, University of California Poet Laureate Award, Gertrude Stein Fiction Award Finalist, *New Millennium Writings* Contest finalist, and Richard Eberhart Poetry Award/*Southeast Literary Review*. A Teaching Professor at Santa Clara University, he serves as Director of the Creative Writing Program and Faculty Advisor to the *Santa Clara Review*. He is co-editor of the anthology *New California Writing 2013*, Heyday.

www.ingramcontent.com/pod-product-compliance
Lightning Source LLC
Chambersburg PA
CBHW020332170426
43200CB00006B/363